Scripture quotations used with permission

Scripture quotations designated ESV are from the ESV® Bible (The Holy Bible, English Standard Version®), Copyright © 2001 by Crossway, a publishing ministry of Good News Publishers.
Used by permission. All rights reserved.

Scripture quotations marked NLT are taken from the Holy Bible, New Living Translation,
copyright ©1996, 2004, 2015 by Tyndale House Foundation.
Used by permission of Tyndale House Publishers, Carol Stream, Illinois 60188. All rights reserved.

Scripture quotations marked TPT are from The Passion Translation®. Copyright © 2017, 2018, 2020 by Passion & Fire Ministries, Inc. Used by permission. All rights reserved. ThePassionTranslation.com.
Scripture quotations designated KJV are from the KING JAMES VERSION, public domain.
Scripture quotations designated WEB are from the World English Version, public domain.

Created by JoDitt Williams / JoDitt Designs
(Any artwork not by JoDitt Williams is used with permission.)

Prayer Journal for Moms & Grandmas:
Guided Daily Prayer Prompts & Scripture Coloring Book Pages
Copyright © 2022 JoDitt Williams | JoDitt Designs
Brighten the Corner Publishing
Stephenville, TX 76401
Available from Amazon.com, and other retail outlets

For other planners & journals, including printable and digital versions, visit:
joditt.com/journals

All rights reserved.
Copy permission: The illustrations/artwork in this book are for personal use only. Permission is granted by author/artist to reproduce pages for small group gatherings of no more than 10 people, such as family gatherings, Bible study groups, Sunday School classes, etc. Any other use, especially commercial use or selling of art - as is, or colored - is strictly prohibited in any form, including digitally or mechanically.

ISBN: 978-0-9983846-5-8

JoDitt Designs
Stephenville, TX 76401
www.joditt.com | facebook.com/jodittw | instagram.com/jodittw

This Journal
BELONGS TO:

_____

BONUS PAGES

At the end of the journal are some bonus pages.

- **Clipart** - Copy this page onto copy paper or cardstock, then cut and paste the images into the margins of this journal or your Bible. You can also color the images if you like.

- **Word Art** - Copy onto copy paper and then trace the words onto the margins of this journal or onto the margins of your journaling Bible. Another option is to copy onto cardstock (or clear sticker paper) and stick onto journal cards, along with your own hand lettering to create your own Scripture memory cards.

- **Coloring Pages** - Color, then cut/tear out page, frame and hang in your home. Or use as tip-ins in your journaling Bible, or use as Scripture memory cards. You can also copy them onto copy paper or cardstock, and then color.

Get FREE Coloring & Creativity
Tips & Tutorials,
Scripture Printables & More at:
joditt.com/delight

Learn more about delighting in the Word of God using color and creativity, on my blog at: joditt.com

HOW TO USE THIS JOURNAL

This prayer journal is divided up into **13 weeks with 6 days per week**. There are two journal pages per day, with an extra page at the end of each week for summary and/or highlights. *You may adapt to fit your schedule as needed.*

Each day, simply fill in the date, and answer the prompts as you have a conversation with God about you as a mother or grandmother, and about your children or grandchildren.

You can write in the journal daily or how ever often you like. You can devote each day to a different child or include prayers for all your children on the same page - do what works best for you.

If the front is an Index so you can write the date and a short note about each doy to make it easier to find entries later.

At the end are pages for you to document answers to your prayers.

INDEX

INDEX, CONT.

DATE:

thank you

WHAT IS YOUR *word* for ME TODAY?

TODAY I CAST THESE *cares* on YOU:

WHAT IS YOUR *word* for _____ TODAY?
(child/grandchild)

scripture for TODAY

STEPS of faith
I CAN TAKE TODAY:

TODAY's PRAYER requests

DATE:

thank you

WHAT IS YOUR *promise* FOR ME TODAY?

THIS IS ON MY *heart* TODAY:

WHAT IS YOUR *promise* FOR _____ TODAY?
(child/grandchild)

scripture
for TODAY

WHAT seeds
CAN I SOW TODAY?

THESE ARE THE desires
of MY HEART:

DATE:

thank you

be WHO DO YOU WANT TO for ME TODAY?

I REPENT, PLEASE forgive ME for:

be WHO DO YOU WANT TO
for _____ TODAY?
(child/grandchild)

scripture for TODAY

what can I believe YOU for TODAY:

I ASK THIS in faith

DATE: _____

thank you

WHAT AM I *afraid* of TODAY?

WHERE AM I NOT *trusting* YOU TODAY?

WHAT *fear* is _____ STRUGGLING with TODAY?

scripture for TODAY

WHAT IS the truth THAT WILL SET ME FREE?

I do believe! HELP MY UNBELIEF concerning:

DATE:

thank you

WHAT IS the *truth*
I NEED to MEDITATE on TODAY?

WHAT *lies*
am I BELIEVING?

WHAT IS the *truth*
I NEED to MEDITATE on TODAY concerning _____ ?
(child/grandchild)

WHAT *lies*
are _____
(child/grandchild) BELIEVING?

scripture for TODAY

I DECLARE THIS truth TODAY:

In JESUS' NAME, I pray

DATE:

thank you

WHAT shall I *focus* on TODAY?

WHAT is *distracting* ME TODAY?

WHAT shall I *focus* on TODAY concerning _____?
(child/grandchild)

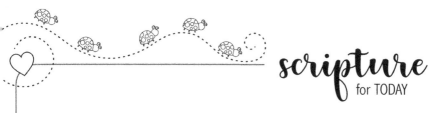

scripture for TODAY

WHAT do I NEED to surrender to YOU TODAY?

LORD, I am trusting YOU with:

PRAISE BE TO THE *LORD,* TO GOD OUR *Savior,*

WHO DAILY *bears* OUR BURDENS.

- Psalm 68:19

DATE:

thank you

WHAT IS YOUR word for ME TODAY?

TODAY I CAST THESE cares on YOU:

WHAT IS YOUR word for _____ TODAY?
(child/grandchild)

scripture for TODAY

STEPS of faith
I CAN TAKE TODAY:

TODAY's PRAYER requests

DATE:

thank you

WHAT IS YOUR
promise
FOR ME TODAY?

THIS IS ON MY
heart
TODAY:

WHAT IS YOUR
promise
FOR _____ TODAY?
(child/grandchild)

scripture
for TODAY

what seeds
CAN I SOW TODAY?

THESE ARE THE desires
of MY HEART:

DATE:

thank you

be WHO DO YOU WANT TO for ME TODAY?

forgive I REPENT, PLEASE ME for:

be WHO DO YOU WANT TO for _____ TODAY?
(child/grandchild)

scripture for TODAY

what can I believe YOU for TODAY:

I ASK THIS in faith

DATE:

thank you

WHAT AM I afraid of TODAY?

WHERE AM I NOT trusting YOU TODAY?

WHAT fear is _____ STRUGGLING with TODAY?

scripture for TODAY

WHAT IS the truth THAT WILL SET ME FREE?

I do believe!
HELP MY UNBELIEF concerning:

DATE:

thank you

WHAT IS the *truth*
I NEED to MEDITATE on TODAY?

WHAT *lies* am I BELIEVING?

WHAT IS the *truth*
I NEED to MEDITATE on TODAY concerning _____ ?
(child/grandchild)

WHAT *lies*
are _____
(child/grandchild) BELIEVING?

scripture for TODAY

I DECLARE THIS *truth* TODAY:

In JESUS' NAME, I *pray*

DATE:

thank you

WHAT shall I focus on TODAY?

WHAT is distracting ME TODAY?

WHAT shall I focus on TODAY concerning _____?
(child/grandchild)

scripture for TODAY

WHAT do I NEED to surrender to YOU TODAY?

LORD, I am trusting YOU with:

PRAISE BE TO THE *Lord,* TO GOD OUR *Savior,* WHO DAILY *bears* OUR BURDENS.

- Psalm 68:19

DATE:

thank you

WHAT IS YOUR *word* for ME TODAY?

TODAY I CAST THESE *cares* on YOU:

WHAT IS YOUR *word* for _____ TODAY?
(child/grandchild)

scripture for TODAY

STEPS of faith I CAN TAKE TODAY:

TODAY's PRAYER requests

DATE:

thank you

WHAT IS YOUR *promise* FOR ME TODAY?

THIS IS ON MY *heart* TODAY:

WHAT IS YOUR *promise* FOR _____ TODAY?
(child/grandchild)

scripture for TODAY

WHAT seeds CAN I SOW TODAY?

THESE ARE THE desires of MY HEART:

DATE:

thank you

WHO DO YOU WANT TO *be* for ME TODAY?

I REPENT, PLEASE *forgive* ME for:

WHO DO YOU WANT TO *be* for _____ TODAY?
(child/grandchild)

scripture for TODAY

 WHAT CAN I believe YOU for TODAY:

I ASK THIS in

DATE:

thank you

WHAT AM I *afraid* of TODAY?

WHERE AM I NOT *trusting* YOU TODAY?

WHAT *fear* is _____ STRUGGLING with TODAY?

scripture for TODAY

WHAT IS the truth THAT WILL SET ME FREE?

I do believe!
HELP MY UNBELIEF concerning:

DATE: _____

thank you

WHAT IS the *truth*
I NEED to MEDITATE on TODAY?

WHAT *lies* am I BELIEVING?

WHAT IS the *truth*
I NEED to MEDITATE on TODAY concerning _____ ?
(child/grandchild)

WHAT *lies*
are _____
(child/grandchild) BELIEVING?

scripture for TODAY

I DECLARE THIS truth TODAY:

In JESUS' NAME, I pray

DATE:

thank you

WHAT shall I focus on TODAY?

WHAT is distracting ME TODAY?

WHAT shall I focus on TODAY concerning _____?
(child/grandchild)

scripture for TODAY

WHAT do I NEED to surrender to YOU TODAY?

LORD, I am trusting YOU with:

DATE:

thank you

WHAT IS YOUR *word* for ME TODAY?

TODAY I CAST THESE *cares* on YOU:

WHAT IS YOUR *word* for _____ TODAY?
(child/grandchild)

scripture for TODAY

STEPS of faith I CAN TAKE TODAY:

TODAY's PRAYER requests

DATE:

thank you

WHAT IS YOUR *promise* FOR ME TODAY?

THIS IS ON MY *heart* TODAY:

WHAT IS YOUR *promise* FOR _____ TODAY?
(child/grandchild)

scripture for TODAY

WHAT seeds CAN I SOW TODAY?

THESE ARE THE desires of MY HEART:

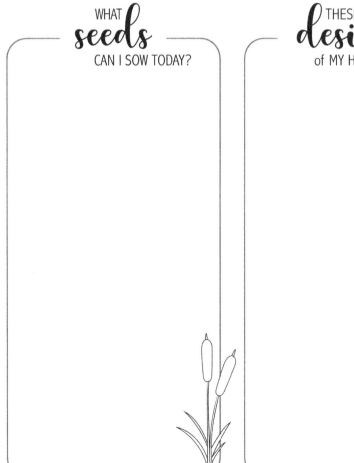

DATE:

WHO DO YOU WANT TO
be
for ME TODAY?

I REPENT, PLEASE
forgive
ME for:

WHO DO YOU WANT TO
be
for _____ TODAY?
(child/grandchild)

scripture for TODAY

WHAT CAN I believe YOU for TODAY:

I ASK THIS in faith

DATE:

thank you

WHAT AM I *afraid* of TODAY?

WHERE AM I NOT *trusting* YOU TODAY?

WHAT *fear* is _____ STRUGGLING with TODAY?

scripture for TODAY

WHAT IS the truth THAT WILL SET ME FREE?

I do believe!
HELP MY UNBELIEF concerning:

DATE:

thank you

WHAT IS the *truth*
I NEED to MEDITATE on TODAY?

WHAT *lies* am I BELIEVING?

WHAT IS the *truth*
I NEED to MEDITATE on TODAY concerning _____ ?
(child/grandchild)

WHAT *lies*
are _____
(child/grandchild) BELIEVING?

DATE:

thank you

WHAT shall I focus on TODAY?

WHAT is distracting ME TODAY?

WHAT shall I focus on TODAY concerning _____?
(child/grandchild)

scripture for TODAY

WHAT do I NEED to *surrender* to YOU TODAY?

LORD, I am *trusting* YOU with:

DATE:

thank you

WHAT IS YOUR *word* for ME TODAY?

TODAY I CAST THESE *cares* on YOU:

WHAT IS YOUR *word* for _____ TODAY?
(child/grandchild)

scripture for TODAY

STEPS of faith
I CAN TAKE TODAY:

TODAY's PRAYER requests

DATE:

thank you

WHAT IS YOUR *promise* FOR ME TODAY?

THIS IS ON MY *heart* TODAY:

WHAT IS YOUR *promise* FOR _____ TODAY?
(child/grandchild)

scripture for TODAY

WHAT *seeds* CAN I SOW TODAY?

THESE ARE THE *desires* of MY HEART:

DATE:

thank you

WHO DO YOU WANT TO
be
for ME TODAY?

I REPENT, PLEASE
forgive
ME for:

WHO DO YOU WANT TO
be
for _____ TODAY?
(child/grandchild)

scripture
for TODAY

what can I believe
YOU for TODAY:

I ASK THIS in faith

DATE:

thank you

WHAT AM I *afraid* of TODAY?

WHERE AM I NOT *trusting* YOU TODAY?

WHAT *fear* is _____ STRUGGLING with TODAY?

DATE: _____

thank you

WHAT IS the *truth* I NEED to MEDITATE on TODAY?

WHAT *lies* am I BELIEVING?

WHAT IS the *truth* I NEED to MEDITATE on TODAY concerning _____ ?
(child/grandchild)

WHAT *lies* are _____ (child/grandchild) BELIEVING?

scripture for TODAY

I DECLARE THIS truth TODAY:

In JESUS' NAME, I pray

DATE:

thank you

WHAT shall I focus on TODAY?

WHAT is distracting ME TODAY?

WHAT shall I focus on TODAY concerning _____?
(child/grandchild)

DATE:

thank you

WHAT IS YOUR word for ME TODAY?

TODAY I CAST THESE cares on YOU:

WHAT IS YOUR word for _____ TODAY?
(child/grandchild)

DATE:

thank you

WHAT IS YOUR *promise* FOR ME TODAY?

THIS IS ON MY *heart* TODAY:

WHAT IS YOUR *promise* FOR _____ TODAY?
(child/grandchild)

scripture for TODAY

what seeds CAN I SOW TODAY?

THESE ARE THE desires of MY HEART:

DATE:

thank you

be — WHO DO YOU WANT TO for ME TODAY?

forgive — I REPENT, PLEASE ME for:

be — WHO DO YOU WANT TO
for _____ TODAY?
(child/grandchild)

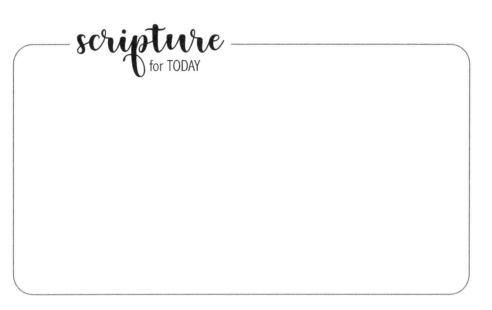

DATE:

thank you

WHAT AM I afraid of TODAY?

WHERE AM I NOT trusting YOU TODAY?

WHAT fear is _____ STRUGGLING with TODAY?

scripture for TODAY

WHAT IS the truth THAT WILL SET ME FREE?

I do believe!
HELP MY UNBELIEF concerning:

DATE: _____

thank you

WHAT IS the *truth*
I NEED to MEDITATE on TODAY?

WHAT *lies* am I BELIEVING?

WHAT IS the *truth*
I NEED to MEDITATE on TODAY concerning _____ ?
(child/grandchild)

WHAT *lies*
are _____ (child/grandchild) BELIEVING?

DATE:

thank you

WHAT shall I focus on TODAY?

WHAT is distracting ME TODAY?

WHAT shall I focus on TODAY concerning _____?
(child/grandchild)

scripture for TODAY

WHAT do I NEED to surrender to YOU TODAY?

LORD, I am trusting YOU with:

DATE:

thank you

WHAT IS YOUR *word* for ME TODAY?

TODAY I CAST THESE *cares* on YOU:

WHAT IS YOUR *word* for _____ TODAY?
(child/grandchild)

DATE:

thank you

WHAT IS YOUR *promise* FOR ME TODAY?

THIS IS ON MY *heart* TODAY:

WHAT IS YOUR *promise* FOR _____ TODAY?
(child/grandchild)

scripture for TODAY

WHAT seeds CAN I SOW TODAY?

THESE ARE THE desires of MY HEART:

DATE:

thank you

who do you want to be for ME TODAY?

I REPENT, PLEASE forgive ME for:

who do you want to be for _____ TODAY?
(child/grandchild)

DATE:

thank you

WHAT AM I *afraid* of TODAY?

WHERE AM I NOT *trusting* YOU TODAY?

WHAT *fear* is _____ STRUGGLING with TODAY?

scripture for TODAY

WHAT IS the truth THAT WILL SET ME FREE?

I do believe! HELP MY UNBELIEF concerning:

DATE:

thank you

WHAT IS the *truth*
I NEED to MEDITATE on TODAY?

WHAT *lies*
am I BELIEVING?

WHAT IS the *truth*
I NEED to MEDITATE on TODAY concerning _____ ?
(child/grandchild)

WHAT *lies*
are _____
(child/grandchild) BELIEVING?

DATE:

thank you

WHAT shall I focus on TODAY?

WHAT is distracting ME TODAY?

WHAT shall I focus on TODAY concerning _____?
(child/grandchild)

scripture for TODAY

WHAT do I NEED to surrender to YOU TODAY?

LORD, I am trusting YOU with:

DATE:

thank you

WHAT IS YOUR *word* for ME TODAY?

TODAY I CAST THESE *cares* on YOU:

WHAT IS YOUR *word* for _____ TODAY?
(child/grandchild)

TODAY's PRAYER
requests

DATE:

thank you

WHAT IS YOUR *promise* FOR ME TODAY?

THIS IS ON MY *heart* TODAY:

WHAT IS YOUR *promise*
FOR _____ TODAY?
(child/grandchild)

scripture for TODAY

WHAT seeds CAN I SOW TODAY?

THESE ARE THE desires of MY HEART:

DATE:

thank you

be WHO DO YOU WANT TO for ME TODAY?

forgive I REPENT, PLEASE ME for:

be WHO DO YOU WANT TO for _____ TODAY?
(child/grandchild)

scripture for TODAY

WHAT CAN I believe YOU for TODAY:

I ASK THIS in faith

DATE:

thank you

WHAT AM I afraid of TODAY?

WHERE AM I NOT trusting YOU TODAY?

WHAT fear is _____ STRUGGLING with TODAY?

scripture for TODAY

WHAT IS the truth THAT WILL SET ME FREE?

I do believe! HELP MY UNBELIEF concerning:

DATE:

thank you

WHAT IS the *truth*
I NEED to MEDITATE on TODAY?

WHAT *lies* am I BELIEVING?

WHAT IS the *truth*
I NEED to MEDITATE on TODAY concerning _____ ?
(child/grandchild)

WHAT *lies*
are _____
(child/grandchild) BELIEVING?

DATE:

thank you

WHAT shall I focus on TODAY?

WHAT is distracting ME TODAY?

WHAT shall I focus on TODAY concerning _____?
(child/grandchild)

scripture for TODAY

WHAT do I NEED to surrender to YOU TODAY?

LORD, I am trusting YOU with:

DATE:

thank you

WHAT IS YOUR *word* for ME TODAY?

TODAY I CAST THESE *cares* on YOU:

WHAT IS YOUR *word* for _____ TODAY?
(child/grandchild)

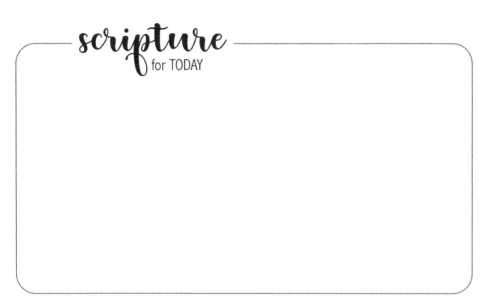

scripture for TODAY

STEPS of faith I CAN TAKE TODAY:

TODAY's PRAYER requests

DATE:

thank you

WHAT IS YOUR
promise
FOR ME TODAY?

THIS IS ON MY
heart
TODAY:

WHAT IS YOUR
promise
FOR _____ TODAY?
(child/grandchild)

scripture for TODAY

WHAT seeds CAN I SOW TODAY?

THESE ARE THE desires of MY HEART:

DATE:

thank you

WHO DO YOU WANT TO *be* for ME TODAY?

I REPENT, PLEASE *forgive* ME for:

WHO DO YOU WANT TO *be*
for _____ TODAY?
(child/grandchild)

scripture for TODAY

WHAT CAN I believe YOU for TODAY:

I ASK THIS in faith

DATE:

thank you

WHAT AM I afraid of TODAY?

WHERE AM I NOT trusting YOU TODAY?

WHAT fear is _____ STRUGGLING with TODAY?

scripture for TODAY

WHAT IS the truth THAT WILL SET ME FREE?

I do believe! HELP MY UNBELIEF concerning:

DATE:

thank you

WHAT IS the *truth*
I NEED to MEDITATE on TODAY?

WHAT *lies* am I BELIEVING?

WHAT IS the *truth*
I NEED to MEDITATE on TODAY concerning _____ ?
(child/grandchild)

WHAT *lies* are _____ (child/grandchild) BELIEVING?

scripture for TODAY

I DECLARE THIS truth TODAY:

In JESUS' NAME, I pray

DATE:

thank you

WHAT shall I focus on TODAY?

WHAT is distracting ME TODAY?

WHAT shall I focus on TODAY concerning _____?
(child/grandchild)

scripture for TODAY

WHAT do I NEED to surrender to YOU TODAY?

LORD, I am trusting YOU with:

DATE:

thank you

WHAT IS YOUR *word* for ME TODAY?

TODAY I CAST THESE *cares* on YOU:

WHAT IS YOUR *word* for _____ TODAY?
(child/grandchild)

TODAY's PRAYER *requests*

DATE:

thank you

WHAT IS YOUR *promise* FOR ME TODAY?

THIS IS ON MY *heart* TODAY:

WHAT IS YOUR *promise*
FOR _____ TODAY?
(child/grandchild)

scripture for TODAY

WHAT seeds CAN I SOW TODAY?

THESE ARE THE desires of MY HEART:

DATE:

thank you

be — WHO DO YOU WANT TO be for ME TODAY?

forgive — I REPENT, PLEASE forgive ME for:

be — WHO DO YOU WANT TO be for _____ TODAY?
(child/grandchild)

scripture for TODAY

WHAT CAN I *believe* YOU for TODAY:

I ASK THIS in *faith*

DATE:

thank you

WHAT AM I afraid of TODAY?

WHERE AM I NOT trusting YOU TODAY?

WHAT fear is _____ STRUGGLING with TODAY?

scripture for TODAY

WHAT IS the truth THAT WILL SET ME FREE?

I do believe! HELP MY UNBELIEF concerning:

DATE:

thank you

WHAT IS the *truth*
I NEED to MEDITATE on TODAY?

WHAT *lies* am I BELIEVING?

WHAT IS the *truth*
I NEED to MEDITATE on TODAY concerning _____ ?
(child/grandchild)

WHAT *lies*
are _____
(child/grandchild) BELIEVING?

scripture for TODAY

I DECLARE THIS truth TODAY:

In JESUS' NAME, I pray

DATE:

thank you

WHAT shall I focus on TODAY?

WHAT is distracting ME TODAY?

WHAT shall I focus on TODAY concerning _____?
(child/grandchild)

scripture for TODAY

WHAT do I NEED to surrender to YOU TODAY?

LORD, I am trusting YOU with:

DATE:

thank you

WHAT IS YOUR *word* for ME TODAY?

TODAY I CAST THESE *cares* on YOU:

WHAT IS YOUR *word* for _____ TODAY?
(child/grandchild)

scripture for TODAY

STEPS of faith I CAN TAKE TODAY:

TODAY's PRAYER requests

DATE:

thank you

WHAT IS YOUR *promise* FOR ME TODAY?

THIS IS ON MY *heart* TODAY:

WHAT IS YOUR *promise* FOR _____ TODAY?
(child/grandchild)

scripture for TODAY

WHAT seeds CAN I SOW TODAY?

THESE ARE THE desires of MY HEART:

DATE:

thank you

be WHO DO YOU WANT TO for ME TODAY?

forgive I REPENT, PLEASE ME for:

be WHO DO YOU WANT TO for _____ TODAY?
(child/grandchild)

scripture for TODAY

believe WHAT CAN I YOU for TODAY:

I ASK THIS in faith

DATE:

thank you

WHAT AM I *afraid* of TODAY?

WHERE AM I NOT *trusting* YOU TODAY?

WHAT *fear* is _____ STRUGGLING with TODAY?

scripture for TODAY

WHAT IS the truth THAT WILL SET ME FREE?

I do believe!
HELP MY UNBELIEF concerning:

DATE: _____

thank you

WHAT IS the *truth*
I NEED to MEDITATE on TODAY?

WHAT *lies* am I BELIEVING?

WHAT IS the *truth* I NEED to MEDITATE on TODAY concerning _____ ?
(child/grandchild)

WHAT *lies* are _____ (child/grandchild) BELIEVING?

DATE:

thank you

WHAT shall I focus on TODAY?

WHAT is distracting ME TODAY?

WHAT shall I focus on TODAY concerning _____?
(child/grandchild)

scripture for TODAY

WHAT do I NEED to surrender to YOU TODAY?

LORD, I am trusting YOU with:

DATE:

thank you

WHAT IS YOUR *word* for ME TODAY?

TODAY I CAST THESE *cares* on YOU:

WHAT IS YOUR *word* for _____ TODAY?
(child/grandchild)

DATE:

thank you

WHAT IS YOUR *promise* FOR ME TODAY?

THIS IS ON MY *heart* TODAY:

WHAT IS YOUR *promise* FOR _____ TODAY?
(child/grandchild)

DATE:

thank you

WHO DO YOU WANT TO *be* for ME TODAY?

I REPENT, PLEASE *forgive* ME for:

WHO DO YOU WANT TO *be* for _____ TODAY?
(child/grandchild)

scripture for TODAY

WHAT CAN I believe YOU for TODAY:

I ASK THIS in faith

DATE:

thank you

WHAT AM I afraid of TODAY?

WHERE AM I NOT trusting YOU TODAY?

WHAT fear is _____ STRUGGLING with TODAY?

scripture for TODAY

WHAT IS the truth THAT WILL SET ME FREE?

I do believe!
HELP MY UNBELIEF concerning:

DATE:

thank you

WHAT IS the *truth*
I NEED to MEDITATE on TODAY?

WHAT *lies* am I BELIEVING?

WHAT IS the *truth*
I NEED to MEDITATE on TODAY concerning _____ ?
(child/grandchild)

WHAT *lies*
are _____
(child/grandchild) BELIEVING?

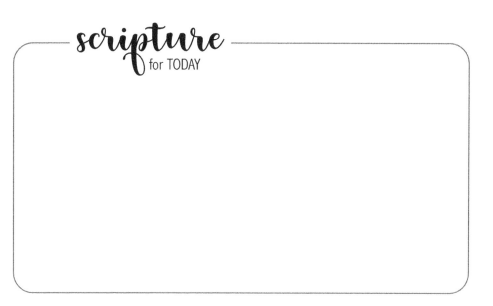

DATE:

thank you

WHAT shall I focus on TODAY?

WHAT is distracting ME TODAY?

WHAT shall I focus on TODAY concerning _____?
(child/grandchild)

scripture for TODAY

WHAT do I NEED to surrender to YOU TODAY?

LORD, I am trusting YOU with:

DATE:

thank you

WHAT IS YOUR *word* for ME TODAY?

TODAY I CAST THESE *cares* on YOU:

WHAT IS YOUR *word*
for _____ TODAY?
(child/grandchild)

I CAN TAKE TODAY:

TODAY's PRAYER *requests*

DATE:

thank you

WHAT IS YOUR *promise* FOR ME TODAY?

THIS IS ON MY *heart* TODAY:

WHAT IS YOUR *promise* FOR _____ TODAY?
(child/grandchild)

DATE:

thank you

be — WHO DO YOU WANT TO for ME TODAY?

I REPENT, PLEASE forgive ME for:

be — WHO DO YOU WANT TO
for _____ TODAY?
(child/grandchild)

scripture for TODAY

believe — WHAT CAN I / YOU for TODAY:

I ASK THIS in faith

DATE:

thank you

WHAT AM I *afraid* of TODAY?

WHERE AM I NOT *trusting* YOU TODAY?

WHAT *fear* is _____ STRUGGLING with TODAY?

scripture for TODAY

WHAT IS the truth THAT WILL SET ME FREE?

I do believe! HELP MY UNBELIEF concerning:

DATE:

thank you

WHAT IS the *truth*
I NEED to MEDITATE on TODAY?

WHAT *lies*
am I BELIEVING?

WHAT IS the *truth*
I NEED to MEDITATE on TODAY concerning _____ ?
(child/grandchild)

WHAT *lies*
are _____
(child/grandchild) BELIEVING?

scripture for TODAY

I DECLARE THIS truth TODAY:

In JESUS' NAME, I pray

DATE:

thank you

WHAT shall I focus on TODAY?

WHAT is distracting ME TODAY?

WHAT shall I focus on TODAY concerning _____?
(child/grandchild)

scripture for TODAY

WHAT do I NEED to surrender to YOU TODAY?

LORD, I am trusting YOU with:

ANSWERED PRAYERS

ANSWERED PRAYERS, CONT.

ANSWERED PRAYERS, CONT.

ANSWERED PRAYERS, CONT.

ANSWERED PRAYERS, CONT.

ABOUT THE AUTHOR

JoDitt Williams is a passionate author, speaker, licensed artist, blogger and entrepreneur on a mission to brighten her little corner of the world and help others do the same.

Whether she is creating art using traditional methods or digitally, her style is always cute, colorful, cheerful and charming.

JoDitt has a passion for encouraging, uplifting and inspiring women to live a life full of joy, while gaining victory over fear. That's why she hosts a monthly Delight in the Word Challenge, and shares about hiding God's Word in your heart through color and creativity on her blog at:
---> **joditt.com**

JoDitt and her husband of over 30 years live in the great state of Texas, where they spend lots of time with their 2 married children and 3 grandchildren.

Join JoDitt's monthly Delight in the Word Challenges at:
joditt.com/ditwmchallenge/

Other Books by JoDitt:
(Available at joditt.com and on Amazon.com)

Delight in the Word of God Volume 1: Favorite Scriptures
- A Devotional Coloring Book & Journal for Adults & Teens

Self-Care Bible Study & Coloring Prayer Journal
- A 4 Week Guided Reading Plan Workbook for Women

Lamb of God Bible Study & Scripture Writing Journal

LEARN MORE AT JODITT.COM

TEST PAGE

Use this page to test out colors, markers, etc.

Made in United States
Orlando, FL
04 May 2022